how to create a legacy bible

AN INSTRUCTIONAL GUIDE FOR PASSING ON FAITH ACROSS GENERATIONS

TRICIA GOYER
LESLIE NUNNERY

STORY ARCHITECT

How to Create a Legacy Bible: An Instructional Guide for Passing on Faith Across Generations

Copyright © 2024 by GoyerInk LLC/Tricia Goyer and Leslie Nunnery

Published in association with Story Architect. www.booksandsuch.com

All rights reserved. No part of this publication may be reproduced, stored in a retrieval system, or transmitted in any form or by any means—electronic, mechanical, photocopy, recording or any other—except for brief quotations in printed reviews without the written prior permission of the publisher.

The website addresses recommended throughout this book are offered as a resource to you. These websites are not intended in any way to be or imply an endorsement on the part of Story Architect, nor do we vouch for their content.

Details in some stories have been changed to protect the identities of the persons involved.

No AI Training. Any use of this publication to "train" artificial intelligence (AI) technologies to generate text is expressly prohibited.

Unless otherwise noted, Scripture quotations are taken from the ESV® Bible (The Holy Bible, English Standard Version®), © 2001 by Crossway, a publishing ministry of Good News Publishers. Used by permission. All rights reserved. The ESV text may not be quoted in any publication made available to the public by a Creative Commons license. The ESV may not be translated in whole or in part into any other language.

Book Cover by Leslie Nunnery

Print ISBN: 978-1-962845-07-6

Printed in the United States of America

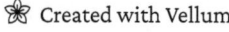 Created with Vellum

dedication

Dedicated to our children and grandchildren.
May God and His Word be your
greatest treasure.

-Tricia and Leslie

Only take care, and keep your soul diligently,
lest you forget the things
that your eyes have seen,
and lest they depart from your heart
all the days of your life.
Make them known to your children
and your children's children.
-Deuteronomy 4:9

MELISSA HANNIGAN

It is a profound experience to reflect and recognize how God is consistently at work, often in ways we least anticipate. In January 2022, I unexpectedly stepped in for Dr. Kathy Koch at a homeschool moms' retreat. Despite feeling unprepared to replace such a popular speaker, the opportunity to visit Panama City, Florida with fellow homeschooling mothers was too good to pass up. This retreat promised a chance to bond with friends and engage with other homeschool moms, encouraging each other on our educational paths. The promise of witnessing beautiful beach sunsets added to the appeal. However, the most significant takeaway from this retreat came from Leslie Nunnery's sharing of a unique tradition.

Leslie introduced me to the concept of a Legacy Bible, a new Bible she would read through, dedicating her reflections and prayers to one of her children. It would be gifted to them on their eighteenth birthday or after their high school graduation. This idea resonated deeply, especially as I considered my soon-to-be-graduating senior. He had felt a calling to ministry, and I believed this Legacy Bible would be a meaningful gift to support him in his spiritual journey, a treasure he could pass down through generations.

Our family decided to embrace this tradition. I envisioned contributions from our youth pastor, small group leaders, and close family friends who had influenced our son's upbringing. This Bible was a compilation of prayers, encouragements, and favorite Scriptures. Little did we know how different our first Legacy Bible experience would be.

On June 6th, 2023, our world was turned upside down when our eldest child, Joey, suffered a paralyzing accident. Despite the devastating prognosis and the challenges of adapting to life with a disability, Joey's unwavering faith and positive spirit were a beacon of hope. He insisted that he could fulfill God's calling for him, even from a wheelchair. His resilience and trust in God's plan were astounding.

Amid this crisis, the concept of the Legacy Bible took on a new dimension. Initially intended as a graduation gift, it became a source of comfort and encouragement through Joey's rehabilitation journey within the ICU. Friends and family, and even hospital staff who witnessed Joey's faith, contributed to the Bible within the walls of the children's hospital. They highlighted Scripture verses and wrote notes and prayers to Joey. Some of the staff, unfamiliar with the Bible, read its pages for the first time. Their handwritten notes and love poured out to Joey were a testament to our son's courage and to God's faithfulness. Even then, none of us realized that this Bible would take on a different purpose than we first imagined.

Tragically, Joey's journey on earth came to an end sooner than we had hoped. Yet, in his passing, the Legacy Bible became a powerful symbol of his faith and his impact on those around him. The stories and verses shared within its pages sparked conversations about faith and God's love, touching the lives of believers and non-believers alike.

Reflecting on the path we've traveled since first hearing about the Legacy Bible, I am reminded of God's sovereignty and the mysterious ways He works. Joey's Legacy Bible, now a cherished keepsake, continues to offer comfort and a reminder of God's presence through the darkest times. It embodies the hope that our children will carry God's Word in their hearts, guiding them on their life's journey.

FOREWORD

As I anticipate creating a Legacy Bible for my next child, I am filled with hope and pray that she will treasure the words and allow them to shape her path. And I pray that Joey's Legacy Bible will serve as a reminder of God's unfailing love and faithfulness, even during profound loss.

-Melissa Hannigan, Author of *Inconvenient Parenting* and mom to Joey, Maddie, Ella, and Charlotte

creating a legacy of faith

TRICIA

In the whirlwind of daily life, moments spent with God often become precious "me" time. He communicates with us during these quiet times, morning or evening, as we delve into our Bibles. Yet, amidst the hustle and bustle, we often miss the opportunity to share these profound faith messages with our children and grandchildren. Imagine the possibility of bequeathing a legacy of faith to your descendants through the pages of a Bible.

Defining a Legacy Bible

A Legacy Bible is essentially any Bible designed with ample margin space for inscribing personal messages and prayers. This allows individuals to pass on their spiritual legacy to loved ones, whether they are children, grandchildren, or friends. These inscriptions allow us to impart our hearts and leave a legacy of faith. While it might seem lofty, picture its impact on your descendants as they discover your reflections and prayers within their Bible. Each entry becomes an invaluable inheritance for future generations.

The concept of a Legacy Bible is not solely our brainchild. Inspired by the idea by people we knew, we each formulated a plan to create such Bibles for our children, customizing the approach to suit our families.

We aimed to leave behind something of significant emotional value, a repository of our words and prayers that could be revisited at any moment. It's about preserving our voices for posterity and establishing a legacy for our children to reflect on during the ups and downs of their lives, even after we've departed this world.

Within this book, the first few sections guide you on your way before you dive deeper into the devotional. When we get to the devotional portion, we share our journeys and guide you to create your own Legacy Bible. There's no better medium to encapsulate our personal faith legacies than the sacred texts of the Bible, where our faith has been nurtured and has blossomed.

Your Bible Can Be Your Legacy

Starting today, your Bible can become a cherished legacy, and this guide will facilitate the creation of your Legacy Bible. Upon acquiring a journaling Bible, you'll find this book to be an invaluable companion, offering a collection of devotions that inspire your entries and motivate you to continue writing. This book is designed to ignite creativity and foster gratitude for God's presence and actions in your life.

In your quiet moments with God, you can write down personal notes that can inspire and encourage future generations. Your handwritten words can convey your love and essence long after you've departed this world. Reflect on the significance of receiving a loved one's note or letter articulating their faith in Christ. Now, envision the impact of a Bible brimming with such faith-focused messages. In our digital age, a handwritten collection of notes and prayers is an invaluable treasure for its recipient.

This devotional aims to inspire you to embark on this journey of legacy by reminding you of God's workings in your life. Each devotion highlights a key Scripture verse and encourages you to annotate your spiritual reflections alongside it in your Bible.

You, like us, undoubtedly have verses that resonate deeply with you—passages that have been pivotal in your faith journey. While this devotional serves as a guide, remember that the Legacy Bible you create is uniquely yours. Every day presents a new opportunity to choose which message to leave behind. You might even begin with verses that mark significant milestones in your life, such as:

1. The moment you accepted Jesus.
2. When a Bible verse profoundly touched your heart.
3. Your reasons for believing in the Bible's relevance today.
4. The narrative of your family's faith across generations.

Leaving a legacy—particularly one of faith, values, and beliefs—often feels abstract. Yet, as we mature and our faith deepens, the essence of our legacy becomes clearer. This *How to Guide* is a tool to transform this intangible inheritance into something tangible by chronicling your words, thoughts, stories, and prayers within a Bible, encouraging you to fulfill this meaningful endeavor.

As you document your stories, reflections, and prayers, you craft a faith legacy to bequeath to a loved one. With each journal entry, you create a treasured keepsake filled with hope and inspiration for future generations. A Legacy Bible is not just a gift. It's a piece of you and a beacon pointing your children toward God, who is eternally present and unwavering in His loving support. Your narrative becomes an integral link to God's grand story. Are you ready to get started?

Our Purpose

This guide is structured with three objectives in mind. First, it encourages you to reminisce and cherish your faith journey. We have all experienced defining moments when we felt God's presence and intervention. It's crucial to acknowledge and document these instances. They are the cornerstone of our faith legacy—narratives worth sharing. And what better way to share them than within the Bible?

Second, this devotional aspires to encourage you to leave a spiritual legacy. Reading through the Bible and adding personal notes can appear formidable. However, this devotional will remind you of the profound significance of your faith legacy by exploring Scripture and stories of others who've endeavored to leave a spiritual inheritance. We will also share glimpses of personal experiences, the challenges encountered, and the joy derived from passing on their faith.

Finally, this devotional will guide the creation of your Legacy Bible, offering practical advice and writing tips. Included are two advisory sections: "Leaving a Legacy Tip" and "Sharing Your Faith Journey Tip." The former provides specific suggestions on selecting a Bible and optimizing its use for creating a Legacy Bible. The latter aids in introspection on your spiritual journey, enabling you to discover avenues to share your experiences within your Bible's pages, thereby crafting a poignant testimony to be treasured and revered by future generations.

After the book, four appendices offer additional support and guidance:

Appendix A: When I Accepted Jesus

This appendix illuminates Scriptures that can be utilized to recount your initial dedication to Jesus within a Legacy Bible. Leslie and I will share insights on capturing these experiences through simple stories.

Appendix B: A Moment When a Bible Verse Changed My Heart

This section encourages you to recall and document significant Scripture verses that have impacted your life, guiding you in how to share these moments in an accessible manner within a Legacy Bible.

Appendix C: Why I Believe the Bible Is Relevant to Me Today

Here, we assist you in recollecting and articulating Scriptures that have recently held particular significance, highlighting the Bible's ongoing relevance in your faith journey.

Appendix D: Our Family's Faith Journey through Generations

This final appendix offers direction on chronicling your family's spiritual history, providing a framework for sharing these stories and illustrating the evolution of faith across generations.

Your Journaling Journey

The journey of your Legacy Bible can commence at any significant moment—following a child's birth, as they begin school, or at any stage of their life. One individual shared with me that she works on several simultaneously, even in her eighties, and has numerous Legacy Bibles to create.

Consider making the Legacy Bible a collective family project, with different members contributing prayers over the years. After all, completing a Bible within a year is not required. Some may choose to document from a child's infancy through adulthood. The timeline is yours to decide. Avoid the pressure of strict deadlines or the need to write on every page. The essence of your messages can be spread throughout the Bible.

Legacy Bibles can be presented on special occasions, such as high school graduations, twentieth birthdays, or wedding days. I gift the Bibles on my children's birthdays the year after completion. Leslie did things differently, preparing Bibles for her children's sixteenth birthdays.

Why Bible Journaling Resonates

Have you ever dedicated time to journaling while reading your Bible? Those who practice this find that pausing to jot down thoughts significantly aids in remembering the readings and integrating the Bible's teachings into daily life.

Journaling invites us to deeply contemplate the text, immerse ourselves in God's Word, and thoroughly process its messages. This active engagement ensures we remain present despite fatigue, distractions, or worries. Writing focuses on pivotal passages, highlighting crucial phrases and fostering a profound connection with

God's Word. Subsequently, the journal entries enable us to craft personal reflections or prayers to share with loved ones. Your Legacy Bible emerges as a conduit across generations, showcasing the relevance of God's Word in your life.

The beauty of journaling within your Bible is threefold. Firstly, it lets you articulate God's message to your heart, offering immediate personal enrichment. Secondly, your documented insights become a tool through which God can reach out to a loved one when they most need guidance. Lastly, when done with a specific individual in mind, creating this gift often brings unexpected revelations as you pray and journal on their behalf, potentially deepening your bond in unforeseen ways.

As you write, you'll find that God guides your heart to the Scriptures most needed, not just for you but for those who will one day cherish your words. The thought that your reflections today could provide solace or inspiration to a family member in the future is a profound blessing. We are thrilled by the prospect of your Bible becoming a bridge between texts and readers and between hearts, utilized by God in remarkable ways.

our stories

How Tricia Began Creating Legacy Bibles

I came into this world as the daughter of a single, college-aged woman, not knowing my biological father's identity until I was twenty-eight. My mother became a Christian when I was seven years old, and the moments spent sitting beside her in church are meaningful to me.

When I met my biological father, he did not share my Christian faith. Imagine my surprise when I meet my biological grandfather a few years later and discovered he was a strong Christian. Not only that, but I found out that I came from a family with a strong spiritual heritage! My grandfather, great-grandparents, and other relatives were pastors, teachers, and missionaries.

I only had the chance to visit my grandfather twice, but during those visits, he passed on to me his Bible, journal, and sermons from himself and his family members. What a beautiful legacy of faith!

After that discovery, I believed the journals and prayer books I would one day leave behind would be a testament to my spiritual journey. I envisioned them being discovered by future generations. Then I considered how much more meaningful it would be if the notes and prayers were individualized. That's when I decided to take on a more deliberate approach. For the last decade, I've dedicated two years to creating a Bible for each of my children, filling them with personalized journal entries and prayers. This tradition will extend to my grandchildren. I desire to pass on my faith through words, creating valued heirlooms for family members.

Through the pages of these Legacy Bibles, I hope to show that Bible reading is more than just "knowing stuff"—it can be a time of personal connection with Jesus. I long to help my family understand how God's Word applies to them. The best part is that, hopefully, as my family members read my notes and prayers, God's Word will also come to life for them. They will understand it better, realize how it applies to their lives, and discover a closer relationship with Jesus.

Where has my dedication to Bible reading led? I have led Bible studies, authored books, founded a crisis pregnancy center, mentored teen moms, and expanded our family by adopting seven children.

More importantly, it's fostered an intimate relationship with Jesus, a legacy I yearn to pass down. The Bible has come to life as I've used journaling to grow my relationship with God. This is the legacy I hope to pass on to my children and grandchildren.

* * *

How Leslie Embarked on Creating Legacy Bibles

Raised in a devout Christian home, my parents' early conversion significantly shaped our upbringing. They ensured that my sister and I had a Christian education and were part of a vibrant church community.

Being in a good church and attending a Christian school didn't do much to strengthen my faith. Sure, God used men and women along the way to mentor and invest in me, and I'm very grateful for that. Yet, looking back, I can't remember a single Sunday school lesson, Bible class, or sermon that strongly impacted my young heart.

What I do remember are conversations with my mom and dad. I understand now that my parents were growing in their faith. As they grew, they brought us along for the journey. So it wasn't the formal lessons but the heartfelt talks with my parents that nurtured my faith.

These discussions were more than just educational. They were transformative, reflecting my parents' spiritual growth and desire to embed that same growth in us. Unbeknownst to them, their legacy was the faith and love they exemplified.

I remember discussing the "whys" behind what we believed or did. I remember their investment of time in knowing us and ensuring they truly connected with our hearts. I remember their faithfulness and evident love of God and people.

My parents passed on a legacy, but I'm not sure they even recognized that as they went along. They were just following step-by-step in the ways God led them, and Kristin and I were the beneficiaries of that.

Journaling became a crucial part of my spiritual discipline at eighteen, a practice that has since filled boxes with reflections on my faith journey. These journals—sometimes embarrassing, yet mostly uplifting—remind me of recurring lessons God has impressed upon my heart.

After marrying David, the conviction that discipling our children was our paramount calling led to the tradition of creating Legacy Bibles. Inspired by a godly elder lady who dedicated a year to praying and note-taking for an individual, I adapted this concept for my children's sixteenth birthdays, dedicating at least a year and a half to each Bible.

Presenting the first Bible to our eldest son was a moment of trepidation, yet his response affirmed the tradition's value, sparking anticipation in his siblings. This practice has not only been a gift for their milestone birthdays but has also deepened my understanding of their hearts and my spiritual growth as I meditate on God's Word with them in mind.

As Tricia and I share this journey with you, we're excited about the transformative work God will accomplish in your heart and family through the discipline of Bible journaling. Are you eager to leave a legacy of faith for your family, friends, and loved ones?

the how-tos of creating a legacy bible

TRICIA

HOW TO START

Begin with a journaling Bible. These Bibles are designed explicitly for note-taking and offer wide margins for journaling—recording notes, prayers, observations, insights, questions, and other reflections on God's Word. Some versions even accommodate artful designs for those who are artistically inclined.

Select a family member to dedicate this Bible to. While choosing just one may be challenging, we recommend creating a single journaling Bible at a time. Ten years ago, I embarked on a journey to create a Bible for each of my children, dedicating around two years to each Bible. Now working on my sixth child's Bible, I use it daily, taking moments after each reading to jot down inspirational thoughts or prayers. Throughout the devotions in this book, we'll share more on how to approach this.

Pray. Prayer is key. Pray for your journey in creating this Bible, for perseverance, and that any doubts you have won't deter your dedication. Pray for the one who will be the recipient of the Bible. Remember, the personal touch counts—perfection is not the goal. Your family members will cherish hearing your heart.

Reflect. Include stories of how God's Word has guided and influenced your life, especially regarding specific Scripture passages. For instance, James 1:27 profoundly influenced my husband's and my decision to adopt, illustrating how the Bible informs our life choices. It reads, "Religion that is pure and undefiled before God the Father is this: to visit orphans and widows in their affliction, and to keep oneself unstained from the world." Adoption is an integral part of our family's story, and sharing how God's Word impacted our decision-making confirms to our children that the Bible applies to every part of our lives. Sharing these moments offers powerful testimony to the Bible's applicability in all aspects of life.

Begin today. By creating a Legacy Bible for each of my children, I ensure a piece of my heart remains with them, providing comfort and guidance even in my absence. The unpredictability of life underscores the importance of not delaying. Having already distributed five completed Bibles, I am creating more. My next step is to create them for my other children and grandchildren, while Leslie has already started working on one for her new daughter-in-law.

The process of creating a Legacy Bible is unique to each individual. It might include writing letters, prayers, sharing stories, or even sermon notes. As I navigate each Bible, I reflect on my children's challenges, embedding my prayers for them within its pages. This lets them see how I've prayed through their triumphs and trials. Reflecting on this process, I see it as a shared journey with God and my children—a truly invaluable gift.

yes, even you can do this!

LESLIE

I never cease to be amazed at the reaction I get whenever this project comes up in a workshop I'm giving or in conversations with other moms. I know Tricia feels the same way. It is a compelling idea, and many parents desire to leave a legacy of faith for their children. Creating a Legacy Bible is a tangible way to accomplish that. This has undoubtedly been one of the most impactful things I've ever done for my children from a discipleship perspective, and it's opened the door for some of the most exciting conversations I've had with other moms.

However, shortly after the initial excitement of the idea hits, parents' questions start flooding right behind it. This is a simple concept, but insecurity and fear stop far too many before they even begin. Tricia and I don't want to see you fall prey to any of the fears or excuses we've heard. I want to answer some of the most common questions or concerns I hear so you can see how doable this project is. This is one of the most personal journeys you'll ever embark on, and I want to encourage you to approach each Legacy Bible you work on in the best way for you at that time.

This approach offers the most effective means of connecting with an individual child's heart through the messages contained in the

Bible. Remain adaptable, allowing yourself to be guided by the Lord throughout the process.

How much time do I need to allow for this project?

Allowing yourself plenty of time to complete the project will keep you from getting mired in perfectionism or allowing setbacks to derail your efforts altogether. What "plenty of time" looks like is as unique as you are. For my children's Bibles, I gave myself two years to write and be able to pass the Bibles around to others who had impacted my children's faith through the years. That worked beautifully at that time in my life, and I could always complete them before their sixteenth birthday. Now, I'm working on a Bible for my daughter-in-law. It's an entirely different experience for me compared to the ones I've done before, and I'm at a season of life where I will be finished with hers in a year.

What if I'm not smart enough to mark a Legacy Bible?

Discipleship is simply leveraging what you've learned on behalf of someone else. So, as you're reading and learning, you can share those things with your children on the page. Before I started my reading each day, I prayed that God would open my eyes and heart specifically to principles that my child and I needed to know. I was amazed at how God grew my faith and understanding of His Word as He also gave me insight into the child I was focusing on, and sharing what I was learning allowed me to leave authentic messages for my children so they can trace my growth through their Bibles.

From time to time, I will share some insight on specific passages to help my children understand them or connect them to other passages. Still, most of what I wrote in their Bibles was about how those principles would be lived out in their lives, how I've seen God's faithfulness in situations that passage reminded me of, how they may experience the truths mentioned in the passage, or to point out things they need to avoid so they don't stumble. You'll also find that the things you're learning as you read through each individual's

Bible give you the right perspective to share your faith and newfound insights with them because God is so faithful to lead us and answer our prayers. It is like an ongoing conversation with the recipient about what God is doing in your life and your hopes, dreams, and prayers for theirs.

What if I'm worried about messing it up?

Since you're sharing from your heart, there's a good chance that not all entries will be as "good" or profound as others. God often uses what we consider "not good enough" in powerful ways, as the timing of our children reading it is perfect for their situation. Scratches, "oops," and other corrections add to the authenticity of what you're sharing. Remember that God takes what we consider a very small offering and magnifies it in His hand. You can trust Him.

Should I share hard personal things?

This is an excellent opportunity to share how God has worked in your life and in your family. Sharing those accounts of God's goodness, even in your failures, is a great way to leverage those lessons you've learned for the sake of others. That's true discipleship. You can help them learn to think biblically as you tie Scriptures to the specific situations you've faced.

How impactful is prayer to this endeavor?

I prayed every day before reading, asking God to show me what I needed to learn, give me insight into that child's heart, and lead me to share something they would need to know in the days ahead. What I didn't count on (and this ended up being one of the biggest blessings of creating these Legacy Bibles) was that as I devoted that time to praying and reading so specifically for one child at a time, God gave me incredible insight into their hearts and strengthened our relationships in ways I would have never imagined.

* * *

What if my child doesn't appreciate it?

Before I gave my oldest son his Bible on his sixteenth birthday, I was concerned he wouldn't appreciate it at that point, but I assumed it would be something he would understand the value of in the future. I was shocked when he did appreciate it and thought it was a fantastic gift. My other kids immediately started asking if they would get one as well. From that point forward, whenever my children would take their Bibles with them to church, camp, etc., their friends would always take notice and note how they wished their moms would do the same thing for them. Our children long for deeper connections with us, even when their actions indicate otherwise. Whether your child shows their appreciation for the gift when it's received or not, trust that the Lord will use it in their life and that they will recognize the preciousness of it in due time.

Should I have others involved in the process?

Allowing others to write in the Bible enriched the final product and constantly reminded each of my children that God has put other mature believers in their lives. Their encouragement and insight blessed me as a mama and showed a deep connection with my children. The way I did it was simple. Once I finished the Bible, I gave it to my husband for a couple of weeks. It was then passed on to my parents and sister. After that, I took it to some select adults in our church community who had invested in that child while they were growing up. The instructions I gave them were as simple as the rest of the project—I simply asked them to share what was on their heart with my child and gave them no restrictions. My dad and mom generally wrote in the middle of the Bible around specific passages they wanted to share about. Most of the others would write a challenge in the front of the Bible. With so many children leaving the church because they don't feel like they have a place there after high school, this can serve as a physical reminder of the relationships they have in the body of Christ.

Do I need to write on every page?

Not necessarily. You need to write the things that you feel you need to share. I read straight through each Bible and wrote as I went. Others have chosen to jump around and drop in their thoughts as they come to them. But not all pages will have your thoughts on them. It's been amusing to me through the years as we have been sitting in church, and one of the kids will look down the row to make a face at me when that page has nothing on it. Their Bibles have a lot of writing, but not every passage inspired me to share with them. I always tell them I left room to put their thoughts on those pages.

Can I create one of these for an unbeliever?

This would be a great outreach to an unbeliever, for it will clearly indicate your love and concern for them. Since you approach the Word daily in prayer, you can expect the Lord to direct how you share your stories and thoughts in that Bible. This labor of love would be a precious gift to give to someone you love who hasn't accepted God's free gift of salvation yet. Because this gift comes from one who loved them enough to pray, read, and write in God's Word, this may be the tool God uses to reach their heart when there is no other witness they'd listen to.

I'm sure I could address more concerns or questions, but you should never forget that "perfect" is the enemy of "done." There's no checklist or "perfect" way to do it, so get started on one now. Give yourself plenty of time and prepare for the Lord to grow your faith and strengthen your relationship with the one you're focused on. It's going to be a fantastic journey!

devotions to encourage you

THE FOLLOWING pages are a small collection of devotions to inspire you. Reading through them isn't a task to be hurried through. Instead, they are an invitation to pause and breathe deeply. These ideas are meant to be read *and* lived. They can unfold and resonate in the rhythm of your daily life.

In the quiet moments amidst the chaos of life, we often find the deepest connection to our faith. Remember, the depth of the journey matters, not the speed at which we travel. Let these be your invitation to slow down, savor, and find a source of enduring strength and comfort in sharing the truth of God's Word with generations to come.

ONE
your bible can be your legacy
TRICIA

> Make me to know your ways, O Lord;
> teach me your paths.
> Lead me in your truth and teach me,
> for you are the God of my salvation;
> for you I wait all the day long.
> -Psalm 25:4-5

LEGACY WASN'T a word I thought belonged to my past until one day when the grandfather I'd only met twice handed me a treasure. Growing up, I didn't know my biological dad. As an adult, I was messaging my sister Lesley, and she mentioned something about Grandpa.

"What? Are you telling me I have a grandfather who's alive?"

Lesley explained that our father's parents divorced when our dad was young, and our father and grandfather weren't close. Lesley passed on our grandfather's information. Within a few months, my family and I traveled from Montana to Washington State to meet him. As I sat in my grandfather's living room, he shared about growing up as a pastor's son. He also explained that most family members were missionaries or pastors. Joy filled me when I learned about this heritage of faith! Even though we'd only known each other briefly, my grandfather focused on leaving a legacy of faith through the stories he shared.

Then, as we were leaving, my grandfather had a few things to give me. He offered me some of the sermons he'd written when he became a church planter in his later years. He also offered me one of his Bibles. I clutched it to my chest as we walked to the car. I couldn't imagine a more beautiful gift. My heart warmed at learning of the legacy of faith passed down through generations—a legacy I was a part of. A legacy I needed to pass on.

Later, as I looked at the underlined passages and notes scribbled in the margins, I saw my grandfather's faith journey. I had physical evidence of how my grandfather sought God's truth and accepted His salvation. I witnessed glimpses of where my grandfather placed his hope, which gave me hope and encouragement to do the same.

From the first few verses of the book of Psalms—and throughout the rest of it—we discover that blessings and happiness are found in those who delight in God's Word. My grandfather's Bible was the best gift he could have given me, and this caused me to consider the legacy I wanted to leave for my children. If my grandfather's notes, written in his quiet time with God, meant so much to me, how much greater would notes written to and for my children mean to them?

Realizing the beauty of leaving a legacy within the pages of a Bible started me on a journey. Since then, I have completed five Legacy Bibles for my children. I am on my sixth Bible and still have four more to go after this one. I hope that, even after I am gone, my prayers and messages to my children will live on through the pages of their Bibles. My grandfather passed away many years ago, but what a joy to still have his legacy of faith written in a Bible that I can turn to time and time again. We may have only met twice, but his story of faith will forever be close to my heart.

. . .

Read Psalm 25
Consider your faith journey. How has God's Word shaped your life? Start by noting down messages you wish to share with your loved ones about God's guidance and faithfulness.

Leaving a Legacy Tip
When creating your Legacy Bible, consider choosing a journaling Bible. These Bibles have extra space for note-taking and journaling. Remember that the purpose of this Bible is to write stories, prayers, and messages within its pages. Don't be afraid to write notes, underline, and highlight in your Bible. Yet don't feel that every note you leave has to be a long prayer or insightful thought. Even a short note that says, "Lord, I pray my child will understand your grace more each day," can be meaningful.

Sharing Your Faith Journey Tip
Sometimes we are afraid to share our faith journey because we don't want our family members to think less of us. But if we talk about how our lives changed "after" Christ, we'll most likely need to share a little about the "before." Our children, grandchildren, and other family members already know we're not perfect. Sharing our mistakes can teach our family how turning to God can bring forgiveness. Consider David's words in Psalm 25:7, "Remember not the sins of my youth or my transgressions; according to your steadfast love remember me, for the sake of your goodness, O LORD!" Even though David made wrong choices, he could point to God's goodness, and we can do the same.

"My husband and I have started Legacy Bibles for each of our children. He is more intentional and consistent than I am. He goes through a Bible each year and writes notes and highlights passages. Our oldest daughter's Bible is complete. We have each given her a Legacy Bible." -Dorinda Blann

TWO

the legacy of faith during hardship

LESLIE

> *For I know the plans I have for you,*
> *declares the* L<small>ORD</small>*,*
> *plans for welfare and not for evil,*
> *to give you a future and a hope.*
>
> *-Jeremiah 29:11*

WHEN MY PARENTS WERE YOUNG, they started a business together. Though I know they made a lot of wonderful memories through that experience, overall it was a very trying time for them. Miraculously, God always sustained them, even as He grew their young faith. Their stories of provision and grace were a testament to God's faithfulness to my sister and me as we grew up.

One Christmas Eve a few years ago, my dad shared this story with us all as we had our family devotion before opening presents.

"In early 1979, Pat and I struggled financially with a weekly newspaper we owned in Kentucky. My heart was not in my work. The stress was almost unbearable, and the financial situation seemed hopeless. At that low point in our lives, we were contacted by a man who wanted to buy our paper. We knew this was the answer we'd been waiting for, and we immediately thought all our problems would soon be over. We went down that path with him until he withdrew his offer at the very last moment. We were devastated. On the way to work, I was praying and asking God "Why?" At that moment, someone came on the radio reading the words to a very old poem. As he read them, I knew exactly why. I pulled over to the side of the road and wept as I realized more fully than ever that God was in control of my life and that He still had plans for me."

What was that poem?

"Disappointment, His appointment. Change one letter, then I see that the thwarting of my purpose is God's better choice for me..."

From that point forward, my parents made sure to give my sister Kristin and me many reasons to put our trust in God, despite the disappointments we encountered. Our parents desired to give us "a future and a hope" as mentioned in Jeremiah 29, even during times when things seemed more wrong than right. This choice became my parents' legacy.

The people Jeremiah was writing to knew disappointment well. They were in captivity in a foreign land. All their hopes and dreams of a promising future were dashed. For these people, the situation they found themselves in was due to their wrong choices. But, even amid judgment, God never left them hopeless—just as He will never leave us hopeless.

Today, you may find yourself in a situation that appears to be without hope, but it never is. In Jeremiah's time, the people were told to build their houses and lives, even in Babylon captivity, and to not pine away after what was lost. Sometimes, our children or grandchildren learn the greatest faith lessons from seeing us live faithfully, even during hard times. This has been true for our family.

For each of us, the greatest legacy stories we leave behind are the ones in which we share how God spoke to our hearts amid our deepest pain and disappointment. Our faith is refined in these moments as we lean into the certainty of God's goodness and His promises for our future. And this is a wonderful message to pass on.

Read Jeremiah 29
Consider your experiences of God's faithfulness amid trials. Sharing stories of God's provision and peace in tough times can become vital to the legacy you leave behind.

Leaving a Legacy Tip
When curating your Legacy Bible, focus on conveying God's promise of a hopeful future to a specific family member. Seek divine guidance to highlight passages that affirm God's plans for them, enriching their understanding of His unwavering support.

Sharing Your Faith Journey Tip
Our journeys are marked by joy and sorrow. Shielding our children from the latter does them a disservice. By sharing our struggles, we demonstrate the strength of our faith and the reliability of God's presence in every season. Encourage your loved ones to recognize God's hand in every circumstance, echoing the awe and gratitude of Psalm 40:5 for His countless wonders and unfathomable plans for us.

THREE

modeling faith

TRICIA

> *This is how one should regard us, as servants of Christ and stewards of the mysteries of God. Moreover, it is required of stewards that they be found faithful.*
>
> *-1 Corinthians 4:1-2*

THERE ARE pivotal moments in life when God calls us to act in faith. My moment came in 1999 with a divine nudge to co-found a crisis pregnancy center in Northwest Montana. The journey from concept to operation—identifying community needs, securing a venue, training, recruiting volunteers, and fundraising—was a testament to faith in action. The Hope Pregnancy Center's opening day marked the beginning of transformative work in our community, offering new paths of hope where once there was fear and uncertainty.

However, amidst this fulfilling work, I grappled with guilt, fearing my ministry might deprive my children of a normal childhood. I especially worried my eight-year-old daughter Leslie. She spent many hours at the center, sorting baby clothes and helping with our teen mom support group. It wasn't until years later that I recognized how this experience was not a hindrance but a foundation for Leslie's future calling.

After college, Leslie was drawn to serve as a missionary overseas. Faced with the need for funds, she chose to rely solely on faith, reminiscent of the early days at Hope Pregnancy Center. Leslie's confidence in God's provision, inspired by our collective experiences of witnessing miracles, was a profound lesson in faith for both of us. Indeed, God's faithfulness to our family became the bedrock of Leslie's journey, affirming the legacy of faith I had inadvertently passed on.

This realization underscores a powerful message for all parents: our actions, rooted in faith, become the blueprint our children may follow. Embedding our stories of faith and dependence on God within a Legacy Bible offers a tangible testament to God's unwavering presence in our lives. These personal accounts of divine guidance and provision can serve as beacons of faith for our children, encouraging them to trust God's plan for their future.

Read 1 Corinthians 4

Consider your journey of faith. Paul's self-description as a servant of Christ invites us to explore our servitude to the divine. Documenting your faith journey in a Legacy Bible preserves your experiences and illuminates the path of faithfulness for future generations.

Leaving a Legacy Tip

What legacy would you like to leave? Write a brief statement encapsulating your desired legacy, and place it where it will serve as a daily reminder of your commitment to imparting a legacy of faith through a Legacy Bible. Remember, the impact of a faith-driven legacy is immeasurable.

Sharing Your Faith Journey Tip

The essence of a Legacy Bible lies not in eloquent writing but in the heartfelt communication of your faith journey. Write as you speak, focusing on sincerity over literary perfection. The value of your Legacy Bible to your loved ones lies in the personal reflections and prayers you share, illuminating God's Word and its transformative power in your life. As it says in Psalm 119:130, "The unfolding of your words gives light; it imparts understanding to the simple."

FOUR
every story has a beginning
LESLIE

> In the beginning God created the heavens and the earth.
>
> -*Genesis 1:1*

EVERY STORY HAS A BEGINNING. When writing a story, the beginning determines whether the reader wants to keep reading. It sets the expectation for what will come in the story's middle and end. It's hard to overstate the importance of opening lines.

We all have found ourselves so wrapped up in a good story that we stay up later than we should—reading, listening, or watching just a little more. Good storytellers have mastered the art of leaving us hanging at a natural breaking point so we'll continue on to the next installment.

In 1996, my grandmother was diagnosed with cancer. We lost her within a couple of weeks of finding out, so the time between her diagnosis and her death was intense. She was endearingly called *Mayme*, and she and I had a very special relationship. I was the first girl born into the family, the oldest grandchild, and I was named after her.

For twenty-three years, I had the privilege of snuggling up to her, calling her often, and hearing her laugh in the way only she could. On the Saturday morning, after we received her diagnosis, I found her on the floor, unable to get up. Because of her weakness and my lack of knowledge, I had no way of helping her stand. Instead, I made us coffee and breakfast, and we sat there on the floor and talked for a couple of hours until my aunt came home and the two of us could help her up together.

I'll never forget the stories she told me that day. Her face lit up as she recounted tales I had never heard before about people who had been gone for a long time. I would have sat there all day just to hear her stories.

Mayme told me things that morning that took us back to when she was a little girl in the small Kentucky town where she lived. I learned the history of families and buildings and heard many funny things that had happened throughout the years that had never seemed worth mentioning. But at that moment, while we sat on the floor in her bedroom, no story felt insignificant, and she shared them all beautifully. I'm eternally grateful for that morning on the floor, for, as God would have it, that would be the last day I'd have a conversation with her. I'm so thankful for those stories and the legacy passed on to me through her words.

The story of creation, and ultimately all of history, has an incredible beginning that kicks off a narrative that none of us would have imagined. The opening line of the Bible is the beginning of the legacy God is passing on to us, and it truly gives us all we need to know about the rest of the story that is to follow.

"In the beginning, God …" God was at work from before time began, and God continues to be at work today. Genesis 1 shows an incredibly detailed account of what happened initially. We see God speaking the world and everything in it into existence. All He created was good.

The opening pages of the Bible are our first glimpse of a God who wants us to know Him. Because of His great love for us, God cared enough to share how creation happened. We see His creativity and power on display, beginning in the first few lines of His Holy Word.

We may have doubts when we sit down to write in a Legacy Bible. We may worry that we won't have enough words. We may question if what we have to share will even matter in the end. Yet just as God cared enough about us to share how creation happened, our words will also display our love. Leaving a legacy starts with words like "Once" or "In the beginning."

When you sit down to work on your Legacy Bible, think about beginnings—the beginning of your life, your faith journey, and your belief in God as Creator and Lord. The beginnings you write about now will help your loved one to know more about your story. Just like I'll never forget my Mayme's tales from her bedroom floor, those you share will make an indelible impression on the one you love.

Read Genesis 1

Do you ever stop and stand in awe that God created everything and told us how it was done? What are some of your favorite things about God's creation? What meaningful stories do you remember a loved one sharing that made you desire to hear more?

Leaving a Legacy Tip

Sometimes, you'll find that what you write may be more like a letter containing hope or help for the one you love as they grow. I've often included such notes throughout my children's Legacy Bibles. Those are personal and practical, and I hope they become a dear treasure to them as they grow older.

* * *

Sharing Your Faith Journey Tip

As I looked back through my children's Legacy Bibles, I was amazed that God gave me very different thoughts and approaches in each of the four Bibles. God cares about the individual to whom you are writing so much that He will direct you as you write to them. Today, you may find that you marvel at the beauty of creation or that God gave us an insider's look at how it happened. Or you may be led to write more of a note compelling your loved one to trust Scripture and believe God's Word as true and inspired. Perhaps you feel led to tell your children how you first learned this story of creation—or share with them a story from their younger days and how they learned it.

There's no wrong approach to journaling in your Legacy Bible. Start with prayer and ask God to direct you as you write in each copy. As we read in Psalm 37:23, "The steps of a man are established by the LORD, when he delights in his way."

"God's viewpoint is sometimes different from ours—so different that we could not even guess at it unless He had given us a Book which tells us such things . . . In the Bible, I learn that God values us not for our strength or our brains but simply because He has made us."

-Corrie ten Boom, *The Hiding Place*

FIVE
for god so loved
TRICIA

> "For God so loved the world, that he gave his only Son, that whoever believes in him should not perish but have eternal life.
>
> -John 3:16

MY MOTHER DEDICATED her life to God when I was in elementary school, and soon after, we started attending a small country church. From that point on, Sunday morning included going to Sunday school. My favorite part about Sunday school was memorizing Scripture verses and receiving a small prize from the cardboard treasure chest. It's amazing how those little things meant so much.

At the time, I was simply excited about candy, stickers, or toys, yet now I know the true treasures were the words of Scripture. As a new Christian, my mother started the legacy of church attendance. My Sunday school teacher also passed on her legacy of faith as she worked with us to memorize Scriptures.

Years later, at seventeen, I found myself pregnant, engulfed in depression and isolation. Despite drifting away from the church during my teenage years, the seeds of truth planted in my heart began to stir. Those Scriptures, a legacy from my mother's dedication to church and Margo's Sunday school lessons, became a beacon of hope during my darkest times.

One particularly low day, feeling forsaken by my boyfriend and friends, I reflected on the joy I once felt in Sunday school. Recalling John 3:16, the first Scripture verse I memorized, reminded me of God's love and sacrifice. It was then that I realized prayer was not just about seeking change in circumstances but in seeking a transformation within myself.

I also remembered the women from my Grandma's Bible study who continued to reach out, embodying the legacy of "loving the least of these." In my despair, I dared to believe God hadn't forsaken me either. A simple, heartfelt prayer marked the turning point toward peace and light in my heart, reaffirming God's love and the promise of eternal life through belief in Him. At that moment, I redefined my faith journey, which began with my mother's path to faith, illustrating the profound impact of passing on faith through generations.

It's a legacy I'm eager to bestow upon my children, teaching them that faith is cultivated in small, consistent steps, like understanding God's love one Scripture verse at a time.

Read John 3

Consider the origins of realizing the need for salvation through Jesus. Who played a pivotal role in passing this legacy to you? Nicodemus recognized Jesus' divine connection through His miracles. What awakened the awareness of your need for God? How can you document this pivotal personal story in your Bible?

* * *

Leaving a Legacy Tip

Consider penning a prayer for your child alongside John 3:16, a universally recognized verse. This prayer can serve as a heartfelt wish for your child to know God and follow Him throughout their life. Let your child know you are committed sharing your story to help strengthen theirs.

Sharing Your Faith Journey Tip

Reflect on the moment you embraced Jesus and committed your life to Him. This story is the cornerstone of the legacy you will share with your children.

Detail the journey leading up to your decision, tailoring the narrative to emphasize that salvation stems from faith, not deeds, as underscored in Ephesians 2:8-9, "For by grace you have been saved through faith. And this is not your own doing; it is the gift of God, not a result of works, so that no one may boast."

SIX

the legacy you pray for will impact your walk

LESLIE

> **FOR YOU KNOW HOW,** *like a father with his children, we exhorted each one of you and encouraged you and charged you to walk in a manner worthy of God, who calls you into his own kingdom and glory. And we also thank God constantly for this, that when you received the word of God, which you heard from us, you accepted it not as the word of men but as what it really is, the word of God, which is at work in you believers.*
>
> -I Thessalonians 2:11-13

"I'm a princess..." That's how my third child answered my question when I asked her about the decision she had just made to accept Jesus as her Savior. I was a little taken aback, wondering if she was just playing around, but she went on. "I'm a daughter of the King."

Even as I think back on that story, my eyes fill with tears and my heart with gratitude. The wisdom I gained from my young child that day was priceless. Though she had wrestled for a while with whether she actually wanted to accept Jesus' gift of salvation, she had made the decision to do so, and she had a very clear view of her new position in Him.

Even before our children were born, David and I had lofty goals for them. We desired that our legacy of faith would be passed on, and this was seen through our prayers. We've always prayed that they would never reject Jesus. We prayed that they would give their hearts and their lives to Him and that He would use them greatly. We prayed that they would stand strong, secure in what they believe, yet remain humble enough to serve.

Since leaving a legacy of faith is important, we have probably prayed similar things for our children hundreds of times. It's hard to imagine any believer who doesn't pray that their children will also come to know and love Jesus. But has that prayer for your children directed your own steps, shaped how you parent, and affected your conversations with your children?

Our prayers for our children—or anyone else for that matter—often have a massive impact on our lives. When we pray that our children will come to know and love Jesus at an early age, we are motivated to present Him to them in as many ways as possible. That prayer may direct your family to prioritize faithfully attending church or to be deliberate in discussing things of the Lord within your home. You're likely to find that the impact of praying for your children will go much further than your years.

As you pray strategically for your children, God will often impress on your heart the need to dive deeper into His Word for yourself. Your prayers and dreams for your children will impact your life daily in countless ways. You'll become aware that to bring them to Jesus, you must also be near Him. To answer their questions, you'll need to know God's Word personally. If you expect them to "walk worthy," as we're called to do, your daily walk must also be worthy. You don't want anything you do to get in the way of their growth.

Isn't God's plan for families amazing? He grows us as parents to be more like Him even as we pray for and lead our children along the way. God's plan is that we leave a legacy of faith, which happens best as we grow in our relationship with Him.

Read 1 Thessalonians 2

How have you seen God's Word take root in your own life and in the lives of those you love? Spend time in prayer today, thanking God for the work He has done within your family. Pray for wisdom and grace as you continue to model what a Christian looks like for your children.

Leaving a Legacy Tip

You'll likely be short on time now and then. In many passages in my children's Bibles, I simply underline or highlight the verses I want them to pay attention to. Sometimes, I would write a couple of words of explanation as to why I was drawing attention to those specific passages, but other times, I just let God's Word speak for itself. It is living and powerful, after all!

Sharing Your Faith Journey Tip

Today's passage helps you leave a legacy by giving you a great opportunity to share with your loved one how you have prayed for them. You could also tell them what your hopes and dreams are for them as they seek the Lord in the days to come. You can share how God has used your prayers for them to transform your Christian walk.

It's exciting to see God at work in your own life. It would be a wonderful idea to keep a running record or journal of the things you don't want to forget after handing off the Legacy Bible. Second Timothy 3:14 tells us, "But as for you, continue in what you have learned and have firmly believed, knowing from whom you learned it." Do what it takes to continue growing in your Christian walk, even after completing your Legacy Bible.

SEVEN
a worthy keepsake
TRICIA

ALL SCRIPTURE IS BREATHED *out by God and profitable for teaching, for reproof, for correction, and for training in righteousness...*

-2 Timothy 3:16

Over the years, I've maintained journals and prayer journals brimming with favorite Scriptures, inspirational quotes, and numerous prayers. Reviewing these journals and witnessing how God has responded to prayers—ranging from the mundane to the significant—bolsters my faith remarkably. These written records, documenting requests from potty training to pressing book deadlines, are tangible evidence of God's active presence in my life.

Initially, I harbored hopes that these journals would someday enlighten future generations about my spiritual journey. However, realism has tempered this expectation. If my children stumbled upon these well-worn pages, would they find relevance in them or even choose to preserve them? Despite my intentions, these journals were primarily for me; their appeal to my children is uncertain. Recognizing this, I've shifted toward a more impactful method of imparting my faith legacy: through a Legacy Bible. This approach ensures that my reflections and prayers, directly addressed to my children, are embedded within the context they most resonate with—God's Word.

My primary aim with the Legacy Bibles is to demonstrate the significance of Scripture in my life. I want my children to engage with the passages I've highlighted and ponder the prayers and notes I've left explicitly to foster their spiritual growth. I envision them recognizing that engaging with the Bible transcends a mere academic pursuit, fostering a profound, transformative relationship with Jesus.

The Legacy Bible is not just a gift. It is a conduit for demonstrating how Scripture can dynamically interact with our daily lives, urging my children and future generations toward a deeper understanding of, and relationship with, Christ. My entries are crafted with the intent of offering guidance, hope, instruction, and a continual return to the profound wisdom of God's Word. The ultimate goal is transformation—both theirs and mine—through the power of Scripture.

Read 2 Timothy 3

Consider the transformative power of God's Word in your journey. Why is it vital to pass this knowledge on to future generations? Recall moments when Scripture profoundly impacted your life and identify stories you can share in your Legacy Bible to inspire and guide.

Leaving a Legacy Tip

Explore your old journals for significant faith milestones, cherished Scriptures, and answered prayers. Use your Legacy Bible to curate a collection of these pivotal moments, offering a legacy of faith in a format that will resonate with and inspire future generations.

Sharing Your Faith Journey Tip

While it's natural to highlight the peaks of our faith journey, consider also sharing the valleys. Reflect on times of struggle or doubt and how you navigated those challenges. Documenting these experiences, along with the Scriptures that provided solace and strength, in your Legacy Bible can offer profound encouragement to your loved ones during their trials, reminding them of the enduring hope and transformation in God's Word. As 1 Thessalonians 5:11 says, "Therefore encourage one another and build one another up, just as you are doing."

EIGHT
servant leadership

LESLIE

JESUS, *knowing that the Father had given all things into his hands, and that he had come from God and was going back to God, rose from supper. He laid aside his outer garments, and taking a towel, tied it around his waist. Then he poured water into a basin and began to wash the disciples' feet and to wipe them with the towel that was wrapped around him.*
    -John 13:3-5

During my high school and college years, I served at The Wilds, a Christian camp in North Carolina. The impact of this experience on my faith and my life's trajectory cannot be overstated. The camp directors emphasized servant leadership, urging us to emulate Jesus.

In the early 1990s, a popular bumper sticker encapsulated a prevailing cultural motto: "He who dies with the most toys wins." This slogan epitomized a widespread ethos of materialism and self-indulgence. However, the camp staff contrasted this worldly wisdom with a profound biblical truth, memorably phrased: "He who dies with the dirtiest towel wins."

This concept captures the essence of the legacy Jesus left for us.

LESLIE

On the eve of His ultimate sacrifice, Jesus chose to perform the humble task of washing His disciples' feet, setting a powerful example of servitude. This act served as a poignant lesson for His disciples and for us, underscoring a stark contrast to worldly values. Jesus' life and teachings call us to a different standard: to love and serve one another, marking us as His followers (John 13:34-35). This ethos challenges us to reflect on our own lives and attitudes. Are we seeking opportunities to serve and demonstrate God's love, or are we caught up in self-serving pursuits? Jesus' act of washing His disciples' feet—including Judas'—invites us to embrace a life of service, transcending selfish ambitions and focusing on the needs of others.

As parents or grandparents, daily life presents countless opportunities to "wash feet"—to serve and nurture the young souls entrusted to us. Reading John 13, we're reminded that true service can be the most impactful legacy we leave behind, embodying Jesus' love in our actions and attitudes.

Read John 13

Consider your role as a servant leader within your family and community. Embracing Jesus' example of humble service brings peace, transforms our relationships, and witnesses to the divine love that motivates our actions.

Leaving a Legacy Tip

Your annotations in a Legacy Bible might vary from personal reflections to expressions of hope for your loved ones. John 13 offers rich teachings on servant leadership and love—ideals you'd want to impart. Even humorous observations on the disciples' personalities, like Peter's eagerness, can make the biblical narrative more relatable and engaging.

. . .

Sharing Your Faith Journey Tip

Reflect on the lessons of servitude you've learned through following Jesus. Matthew 5:16 says, "In the same way, let your light shine before others, so that they may see your good works and give glory to your Father who is in heaven." Sharing these experiences can inspire your loved ones to embrace a life of service, shining God's light in the world. Live so that others are drawn to glorify God through witnessing our deeds, a testament to the transformative power of living out our faith.

NINE
a legacy of prayer
TRICIA

I love the Lord, for he has heard my voice and my pleas for mercy.

-Psalm 116:1

ONE OF MY favorite stories about the legacy of prayer concerns Corrie ten Boom, a woman whose family lived in the Netherlands and sheltered Jews during World War II. For her efforts to hide Jews from arrest and deportation during the German occupation of the Netherlands, Corrie was recognized as one of the "Righteous Among the Nations" by the Yad Vashem, Holocaust Martyrs' and Heroes' Remembrance Authority. Yet Corrie paid dearly for her compassion. Because of their work sheltering Jews, Corrie and other family members were imprisoned by the Nazis. Corrie was the lone survivor, being released from the Ravensbrück Concentration Camp due to a clerical error.

The ten Boom family's commitment to prayer began generations before Corrie's time, initiated by her grandfather, Willem ten Boom, who felt compelled to pray for Jewish people after a poignant worship service. This led to weekly prayer meetings starting in 1844, focusing on the peace of Jerusalem, as encouraged in Psalm 122:6. These gatherings continued for a century, ceasing only when Nazi forces arrested the family. This century-long prayer vigil is a testament to the enduring impact of intercessory prayer across generations.

Reflecting on Corrie's legacy inspires me as I compile Legacy Bibles for my family. Embedding prayers within these Bibles, I'm reminded of the unknown future my descendants will navigate, bolstered by the thought that my prayers might fortify them against unforeseen challenges, much like Corrie was by her family's prayers.

Prayer transcends time, reaching out to God for both present and future generations. As we document our prayers in the margins of a Legacy Bible, we intercede for our children and grandchildren and model a life of prayerful reliance on God.

Read Psalm 116

Consider the models of prayer in your life. The example we set can significantly influence our descendants' spiritual journeys, emphasizing the importance of being prayerful role models. Let us pray for the grace to exemplify a life of prayer, understanding that our intercessions could have ripple effects through generations.

Leaving a Legacy Tip

Incorporating prayers into a Legacy Bible offers a dual opportunity: to address immediate concerns facing our loved ones and to inscribe timeless petitions for their spiritual welfare. It's comforting to think that, one day, they might find solace or guidance in our written prayers, a testament to the power and foresight of our love for them.

. . .

Sharing Your Faith Journey Tip

Utilize today's Scripture as a springboard to share personal stories of answered prayers with your loved ones. Whether it was a swift response or a decades-long wait for God's intervention, these stories underscore the vitality of prayer in our lives, encouraging our children to weave prayer into the fabric of their own experiences.

TEN
longing for god
LESLIE

As a deer pants for flowing streams, so pants my soul for you, O God.

-Psalm 42:1

IN MAY OF 2019, our family had the privilege of taking an epic ten-day trip to Israel. Our goal was for the Bible to come alive so we would better understand the legacy of the faith family we're a part of. That trip was life-changing for all six of us. We toured the land where Jesus walked and where most things we learned about in God's Word happened. Seeing the landscape and better understanding the culture expanded our understanding of God's Word in amazing ways, and we are all grateful that God made a way for us to go.

In the middle of that trip, our tour group headed south toward the Dead Sea from the Sea of Galilee, where we had spent a few days. As we drove, we were amazed at the stark difference in landscape from the beautiful, lush countryside in the north to the mountainous desert of the South.

It was there that Psalm 42:1 became even more real to me. We stopped to visit Ein Gedi, a beautiful oasis in the mountains where David and his men hid from King Saul. While it's easy for us to remember David's legacy as a man of faith, we should also remember him as someone who turned to God during times of hardship.

We were almost overwhelmed by the heat when we got off the bus that day. The sun was high, and there wasn't a cloud in the sky to offer any break from the intense rays. On the hike to return to the oasis, we walked between dry, rocky cliffs that towered above us on both sides. Before long, we noticed tiny deer around us, jumping nimbly on narrow rock pathways as they ascended the hills.

Our first question was, "How on earth could those little deer survive there?" It was so intensely hot and so dry. That's when God brought this verse to mind, and I stood in awe of its powerful imagery. Those deer would have died in the relentless dry heat if they had stayed still. They had to be constantly moving, searching for a water source to cool and relieve them. They risked their lives by being exposed to predators in their search for that life-giving water, and when they found it, they'd do whatever it took to stay nearby. And in that moment, the legacy of David's words came to life, "As the deer longs for streams of water . . ."

The world in which we live is spiritually dry and barren. There are hard things that come into all our lives, but God has graciously given us a constant source of refreshment for our weary, parched souls through His Word. Like those deer near Ein Gedi, we all need to do whatever it takes to stay close to that source of refreshment. As we work on leaving a legacy through these Bibles, we can be an example to our children even during hard times. We can remind our children how our souls can be refreshed, even through life's challenges, as we turn to God and His Word.

* * *

Read Psalm 42

Do you find yourself longing for God like those deer long for the waters they had hunted for? Have you developed an insatiable thirst for God's Word, or are you trying to fill yourself with lesser things? Today, pray that God will give you a thirst to know Him more and to draw nearer to Him daily.

Leaving a Legacy Tip

"Remember when . . . " That's how the inscription for this passage starts in my younger daughter's Bible. Tying biblical passages to personal experiences you've shared with your child can help bring that passage to life in a brand-new way. Ask God to remind you of "remember when" situations you can share with your child as you create her Legacy Bible.

Sharing Your Faith Journey Tip

The passage we read today allows you to share with the ones you love about a time you found yourself in a particularly dark and dry place. Share how God worked to bring you out of that place and what you learned along the way. Our children need to hear about our struggles, or they will miss out on hearing the lessons God taught us in those valleys.

As we allow difficulties to drive us to God's Word, we begin to know God better, for we see His character revealed throughout. The more we know Him, the more we understand that we can trust Him. In 2 Peter 1:3-4, He tells us that He has given us "all things that pertain to life and godliness" and that "he has granted to us his precious and very great promises, so that through them you may become partakers of the divine nature." Not only can we know God better by being in His Word, but we will also find that we become more like Him as we do. God never wastes those dry times—use those times to share your legacy.

ELEVEN
strength that overcomes evil

TRICIA

"And do not be grieved, for the joy of the LORD is your strength."

-Nehemiah 8:10

GROWING up in the South as a young black girl in the 1950s wasn't easy, especially in Little Rock, Arkansas. Yet by the time she was three, Melba Pattillo Beals knew the 23rd Psalm by heart. It was the first thing she memorized and the first thing she learned to write. While Melba's grandmother, India, taught her only to use the bathrooms marked for blacks and to be happy with the secondhand books in the segregated school, she knew that God's Word would prepare Melba more than anything else.

In 1957, Melba was selected as one of the "Little Rock Nine." This title was given to the nine African American students chosen to integrate the previously all-white Central High School. When the nine students showed up for the first day of school, their entrance was blocked by the Arkansas National Guard, which the governor of Arkansas sent. It was only when, three weeks later, President Eisenhower sent the 101st Airborne Division that the students were allowed to attend classes.

Only fifteen years old, Melba learned to lean on God as never before as she stood up against heartbreaking injustices and harassment that school year. And when it came to moving from class to class, Melba was able to ignore the verbal and physical abuse by reciting God's Word. She discovered that she could recite Psalm 23 twelve or thirteen times between classes, depending on how fast she walked. "Even though I walk through the darkest valley, I will fear no evil, for you are with me," she'd say repeatedly.

In addition to leaving the legacy of memorizing Scripture, Melba's grandmother told her daily, "God is as close as your skin, and you have only to call on Him for help." This reminder guided Melba through that year of high school and through many hard days to come. Her heart found encouragement during numerous hardships through the truth that God's presence was always with her.

Now eighty-two years old, Melba continues to share how the legacy of faith that her grandmother passed down impacts her every day. Through books and speaking, she wants people to know that while she could be considered heroic, God's Word in her heart made all the difference. We can teach our children this truth: though we never know what they will face, God's Word can prepare them for whatever may come.

Read Nehemiah 8

Do you find yourself too busy to memorize God's Word and teach it to your children? In Nehemiah 8, the people asked Ezra to bring out the Book of the Law of Moses. Seeing God's Word exalted, the people praised the Lord. Hearing the Law, they wept as they began to understand the passages. Yet it was then that Nehemiah told the people that the joy of the Lord would be their strength. Today, pray that God will give you a desire to memorize God's Word with your children. Through the joy of the Lord and knowing

God's Word, your children will find strength for whatever will come.

Leaving a Legacy Tip

What is a special verse you memorized as a child or even as an adult? Find that verse in your Bible. Did anyone help you memorize that verse? Then, write about what that verse means to you now.

Sharing Your Faith Journey Tip

I learned about Melba's story when I first visited the Central High School Museum in Little Rock, Arkansas. I later read many of her books, including *Warriors Don't Cry*. I've even talked to Melba numerous times over the phone. Even though I've never lived anything like what Melba experienced, her story has affected me. While it's important to share our stories with our children, we can also share the faith stories of others. When our children hear the faith legacy of others, they can learn to also trust God during the times they "walk through their darkest valleys."

TWELVE

a faith that grows

TRICIA

> *"God will provide for himself the lamb for a burnt offering, my son."*
>
> *-Genesis 22:8*

THERE ARE NO PERFECT FAMILIES. I'm glad the Bible highlights this. Of all the people God could have picked as the father of His chosen people, God chose a man named Abram. Abram's name was later changed to Abraham, which means "father of many." The problem was that Abraham had no children with his wife, Sarah. To resolve this, Sarah (then called Sarai) suggested he have a child with her Egyptian maid, Hagar. Much later, after God confirmed His promise to Abraham, Isaac was born to Sarah. Yet that's not the end of Abraham's faith being tested.

God later tested Abraham's faith by asking him to sacrifice his promised son, Isaac. We know the end of the story, but picturing the scene as Abraham and Isaac head up into the mountains to offer a sacrifice makes me imagine background music for a B-rated horror film. The two walk together to offer a sacrifice to God, and the only living thing with Abraham is his son! Isaac questions this—and for good reason. But Genesis 22:8 sums up Abraham's growing faith as he tells Isaac, "God will provide for himself the lamb for a burnt offering, my son." Unlike his decision to have a child with Hagar, Abraham had faith in God's provision this time, even before he saw the answer. Abraham had learned to trust God to provide, and he wasn't disappointed. A ram stuck in the thicket became the sacrifice.

Each of us has a faith journey, and our experiences teach us to trust God. Sometimes, we learn to trust Him when we see our prayers answered. Other times, our trust grows when we make mistakes and witness God's faithfulness.

I have made mistakes, as I know you have. Sometimes, we may feel we have to hide these errors in judgment from our children. Instead, our mistakes can be part of our faith legacy. We can encourage our children when they make mistakes by sharing how our faith has grown, just like Abraham's. Our not-so-perfect faith journey can encourage our children to trust God in new ways.

Read Genesis 22

Do you ever wonder how your walk of faith impacts your children? Sometimes, we worry that we've messed up too much for God to use us. Other times, we try to trust God, but things don't turn out as we had hoped. The good news is our faith can grow and encourage our children.

Abraham left a legacy of faith for Isaac, but not because Abraham did everything right. Instead, he left a legacy of faith even after he got things wrong. He grew in his trust in God, and his example taught Isaac to do the same. Today, pray that God will use your faith journey for good. Through your growing faith and your children reading about your faith, your children can learn to trust God, even when they don't get it right the first time.

. . .

Leaving a Legacy Tip

Think about an instance in which you learned to trust God in a new or different way. Use Abraham's story as a launching point for writing about your growing faith within the pages of your Legacy Bible.

Sharing Your Faith Journey Tip

Through the ups and downs of Abraham's life, he learned to trust in God's provision. Provision is "a supply that is prepared in advance." Even though it's hard to believe, God knows our needs before we do. He has a supply prepared in advance, even when it doesn't feel like it.

God is faithful, and as we trust Him, we grow in faithfulness. Later, Abraham is seen as being faithful by his descendants—not because of how he started, but because of where he ended up. Hebrews 11:8-10 says, "By faith Abraham obeyed when he was called to go out to a place that he was to receive as an inheritance. And he went out, not knowing where he was going. By faith he went to live in the land of promise, as in a foreign land, living in tents with Isaac and Jacob, heirs with him of the same promise. For he was looking forward to the city that has foundations, whose designer and builder is God."

No one has a perfect faith walk. Sharing how far we've come can encourage our children, just as Abraham's growing faithfulness encourages us today.

closing thoughts

LESLIE

I had no idea how God would use this idea when I started writing my first Legacy Bible about ten years ago. Now, though, I can honestly say that the hours I've spent creating Legacy Bibles for my children have been among the most impactful moments in my walk with God and in the discipleship of my children. I looked forward to picking up their copy of God's Word each morning, and I enjoyed the excitement the younger ones had, knowing I was working on their Bible.

Each one I've done has been entirely different from the others, and I can even trace my growth in Christ and as a mother as I look back through them now. The inscriptions inside them have opened the door for many conversations with my children that I may have never had the opportunity or insight to have otherwise, as the kids have come across things I've written that pique their interest or make them think in a whole new way. I'm so grateful that God led me to begin this tradition, and I'm eager to see you embark on this journey yourself.

The insight you'll gain into the heart of the person you're writing for will amaze you. How God uses what you're learning as you read through His Word on behalf of another will encourage you to keep digging deeper, praying more intentionally, and walking with Him, come what may. Knowing you've left a legacy of how God has worked in your own life and how you pray He works in theirs will deepen your relationship with the recipient and increase your gratitude for the great things God has done in both your lives.

So grab a Bible and a pen and get started now. You'll never regret it! Don't allow perfectionism, fear, or insecurity to hold you back. Go into the project without trying to make it look like anything. God will direct what you write as you seek His face for the project and make it as unique as you are.

Pray each day as you open the Bible, asking God to give you insight into the heart and needs of the recipient. Give yourself plenty of time to work through the Bible—even if that means you don't get it done by your initial deadline. God knows when the impact of the gift will be most profound for your child, so allow Him to lead you, even in the timing.

No matter what format it takes, the one for whom you're writing will be blessed with a lasting record of the legacy of faith you left behind for them. What a treasure that will be!

WHEN I ACCEPTED JESUS

In this appendix, we aim to guide how you can illuminate the Scriptures that were instrumental in your initial dedication to Jesus. This part of your Legacy Bible is not just a record of verses; it's a deeply personal account of your faith journey.

Understanding the Importance

The act of accepting Jesus into your life is a pivotal moment for many believers. It marks the beginning of a transformative journey, a step into a life guided by faith, love, and the teachings of Christ. Recording this in your Legacy Bible is a testament to your faith and a beacon for future generations to understand and draw inspiration from.

Selecting Scriptures

When choosing Scriptures to include, reflect on the verses that spoke to you during your moment of acceptance. These might be verses that provided comfort, offered guidance, or ignited a sense of hope and renewal within you. Some individuals love the simplicity and profound promise of John 3:16. Others are moved by the personal call to discipleship in Matthew 16:24. Consider also including psalms that reflect your gratitude and awe in experiencing God's grace.

Sharing Insights

Leslie and I encourage you to delve beyond merely listing verses. Share your insights on why these Scriptures are significant to you. What did they reveal about God's character? How did they change your understanding of faith? This narrative layer adds depth, making your Legacy Bible a rich resource of personal testimony and divine truth.

Simple Storytelling

Your story doesn't need to be complex or written with eloquent prose. The power lies in authenticity and simplicity. Start with the context of your life at the time you accepted Jesus. What were you seeking? What struggles were you facing? Then, narrate how you encountered God's Word and its impact on you. Conclude with the changes you've experienced since then, both in your inner life and in your actions.

Practical Tips

1. Start with Prayer: Before writing, pray for guidance and clarity. Ask God to help you recall and articulate your experiences in a way that honors your journey and His work in your life.

2. Be Honest and Vulnerable: Authenticity touches hearts. Don't shy away from sharing your doubts, fears, and the transformative power of grace in overcoming them.

3. Use Simple Language: The goal is to communicate effectively, not to impress. Simple, clear language ensures your story is accessible to everyone, including younger generations.

4. Incorporate Reflection Questions: At the end of your note, consider adding a few questions that encourage your child's reflection. For example, "What scriptures have touched your heart deeply?" or "How do you see God's hand in your life's pivotal moments?"

A Legacy Bible is a beautiful way to document your spiritual foundation. It's an opportunity to consider where your journey with Christ began and to share that story with others. Through this process, you not only preserve your legacy of faith but also inspire others to explore their relationship with God. Remember, each story is unique, and it's in these personal accounts that the universal truth of God's love and salvation shines brightest.

A MOMENT WHEN A BIBLE VERSE CHANGED MY HEART

In this appendix, we focus on the profound impact that Scripture can have on an individual's heart and life. It's about those moments when a verse from the Bible speaks directly to you, offering insight, comfort, or a challenge that leads to a significant change within. Within the pages of your Legacy Bible, sharing these stories personalizes your faith journey and serves as a testament to the living and active nature of God's Word.

Recognizing the Impact

Scripture can transform hearts and minds, guiding us through life's complexities with wisdom and grace. A verse that changed your heart might have come to you in a time of need or during a moment of reflection, altering your perspective, deepening your faith, or inspiring a new path. These entries in a Legacy Bible are dedicated to those pivotal moments, capturing how God's Word has been a lamp to your feet and a light to your path (Psalm 119:105).

Identifying Your Verses

Begin by identifying the verses that have had a significant impact on your heart. These might be verses that provided solace during trials, offered forgiveness when you felt unworthy, or called you to a higher purpose. The verses could range from promises of God's presence, like Isaiah 41:10, to calls for action, like Micah 6:8. Reflect on the circumstances and the changes these verses ignited in your life.

Sharing Your Story

Once you've selected a verse, share the story of its impact on you. Describe the situation you were in when this verse became pivotal. What were you feeling? What challenges were you facing? How did this verse come to you? Was it during a sermon, a personal Bible study, or perhaps shared by a friend? Then, delve into how this verse changed your heart. Did it bring about a new understanding, a change in behavior, or a deeper relationship with God?

Simple Storytelling Tips

1. Be Concise: Keep your stories focused and to the point. A powerful moment doesn't need a lot of embellishments to be impactful.

2. Be Relatable: Share your story in a way that others can relate to, showing your vulnerability and the genuine change that occurred.

3. Be Specific: Detail how the verse specifically impacted your heart and life. This specificity will help others see the practical effects of Scripture.

4. Reflect Deeply: Spend time in prayer and reflection to accurately recall and articulate the moment and its impact on you.

5. Write from the Heart: Let your narrative flow naturally. The authenticity of your experience will speak louder than the most eloquent words.

6. Encourage Interaction: At the end of your story, encourage readers to reflect on their moments of change due to Scripture. You might pose questions like, "Have you experienced a similar moment with God's Word?" or "What verse has profoundly affected your journey?"

APPENDIX B

Your reflections are more than just a collection of personal anecdotes; they celebrate the transformative power of God's Word in our lives. By sharing these moments, you document your spiritual milestones and offer encouragement and inspiration to those who may read your Legacy Bible in the future. These stories remind us all that Scripture is alive, capable of touching hearts, and changing lives today just as it has throughout history.

appendix c
WHY I BELIEVE THE BIBLE IS RELEVANT TO ME TODAY

In this appendix, we explore the timeless relevance of the Bible and its profound applicability to our lives in the contemporary world. Despite the millennia that separate us from the events and teachings recorded in Scripture, its truths remain universal, offering guidance, comfort, and wisdom for the challenges we face today. This section of your Legacy Bible is an invitation to reflect on and share the Scriptures that have resonated with you in recent years, illustrating the enduring connection between God's Word and the everyday experiences of His people.

The Timelessness of Scripture

The Bible—a collection of writings spanning centuries, cultures, and languages, addresses the fundamental aspects of human experience—faith, hope, love, loss, and redemption. Its enduring relevance lies in its ability to speak to the human condition, offering insights that transcend time and culture. By sharing why you believe the Bible applies to your life today, you affirm the Word's living and active nature (Hebrews 4:12), demonstrating its capacity to guide, transform, and uplift.

Identifying Meaningful Scriptures

Start by identifying the Scriptures that have been particularly meaningful to you in recent years. These might be verses that have guided you through personal challenges, offered hope in difficult times or illuminated your understanding of God's will. Perhaps Philippians 4:13 has empowered you to face adversity, or James 1:5 has encouraged you to seek wisdom in decision-making. Reflect on the moments when Scripture has felt especially relevant, and consider what these verses reveal about God's presence and promises in your life.

Sharing Your Insights

For each scripture you select, share your insights on why and how it applies to your life today. Describe the circumstances or challenges that made these verses stand out. What was happening in your life or the world around you? How did these scriptures offer perspective, comfort, or direction? Your insights will not only provide a personal testimony to the power of God's Word but also encourage others to see its relevance in their own lives.

Practical Tips for Sharing

1. Personal Reflection: Begin with personal reflection and prayer, asking God to highlight the verses that have been most significant to you recently.

2. Contextualize the Relevance: Offer a brief context for each Scripture's impact.

3. Illustrate with Stories: Share a specific story or example illustrating the scripture's applicability. This narrative approach makes your insights more relatable and compelling.

4. Encourage Engagement: Invite your child to reflect on their experiences within the Bible. Encourage them to consider how Scripture speaks into their lives today and to share these insights with others.

APPENDIX C

By sharing the Scriptures that have been especially meaningful to you in recent years, you offer a testament to the Bible's ongoing relevance and power to guide, comfort, and challenge us, no matter our circumstances. This personal reflection not only enriches your faith journey but also serves as a beacon of hope and truth for future generations who encounter your Legacy Bible.

OUR FAMILY'S FAITH JOURNEY THROUGH GENERATIONS.

Connecting Family Stories with Scripture

Incorporate personal and family stories into your Legacy Bible to intertwine the narrative of your family's faith journey with the foundational truths found in Scripture. Here's how to create a deeply personal and spiritually significant record:

Understanding the Journey

Your family's faith journey is a unique saga marked by moments of profound belief, significant trials, spiritual transformations, and divine blessings. It encompasses how ancestors embraced the faith, overcame obstacles due to their beliefs, established meaningful traditions, and passed on the faith. Highlighting these spiritual milestones in your Legacy Bible not only honors your predecessors but also demonstrates the timeless relevance of faith.

Gathering Stories

Commence by collecting stories from family members and through historical records that highlight your family's spiritual heritage. Focus on key events like conversions, impactful life deci-

...ade in faith, spiritually significant traditions, and instances which faith provided solace and strength.

Structuring Your Narrative

Shape your narrative to seamlessly weave personal and family stories with Scripture, organizing it to reflect the chronological faith journey of your family. Include:

1. Introduction: Summarize your family's faith background, setting the context for the following personal journal entries.

2. Generational Narratives: Document the faith stories of each generation, emphasizing the spiritual lessons learned, the challenges faced, and how God's faithfulness was evident in each situation.

3. Spiritual Traditions: Share the origins and meanings behind your family's spiritual traditions, linking them to relevant scriptures that underscore their significance.

4. Personal Reflections: Use journal entries to reflect on how these stories and traditions have shaped your faith and life practices.

5. Scriptural Connections: For each story or tradition, pair it with corresponding scriptures highlighting God's truths and promises relevant to shared experiences.

6. Future Generations: Craft entries as letters or messages to future generations, sharing insights and encouragements stemming from your family's history and the timeless wisdom of Scripture.

Practical Tips

1. Engage in Conversations: Don't wait to capture family stories —initiate discussions about faith experiences within your family to uncover stories that may be interwoven with Scriptural insights.

2. Preserve Memories: Consider recording or writing down these discussions as direct quotes in your Bible, ensuring authenticity and a personal touch.

3. Inclusive Narratives: Make an effort to include a wide range of stories from different family members to capture the breadth of your family's faith journey.

By weaving personal and family stories with Scripture in your Legacy Bible, you create a rich tapestry that not only pays tribute to your ancestors' faith journeys, but also highlights the continuing relevance and power of God's Word in daily life. This personalized Bible serves as a spiritual heirloom, offering wisdom, strength, and guidance for future generations rooted in the enduring promises of Scripture.

connect with tricia and leslie

Tricia Goyer is a distinguished author and speaker within the Christian community, celebrated for her profound contributions to Christian fiction, non-fiction, and family life. As an acclaimed author, she has penned over 90 books, including notable titles such as *Heart Happy: Staying Centered in God's Love Through Chaotic Circumstances* and *The Grumble-Free Year: Twelve Months, Eleven Family Members, and One Impossible Goal*, showcasing her versatility and depth in exploring themes of faith, resilience, and family dynamics. Tricia's writing journey reflects a heartfelt mission to inspire and uplift, drawing from her own experiences as a mother of ten and a grandmother, to offer wisdom and encouragement to families navigating the complexities of modern Christian living. Beyond her literary achievements, Tricia Goyer is a respected voice in the Christian homeschooling movement, offering invaluable insights and support to parents through her blog, workshops, and public speaking engagements. Her commitment to faith, family, and community resonates deeply with her audience, making her a beloved mentor and guide for those seeking to deepen their faith and strengthen their family bonds in accordance with Christian values.

Discover all of Tricia's books at https://www.TriciaGoyer.com

Popular Books by Tricia Goyer

Heart Happy: Staying Centered in God's Love Through Chaotic Circumstances

The Grumble-Free Year
Prayers That Changed History
Praying for Your Future Husband: Preparing Your Heart for His
Walk It Out: The Radical Result of Living God's Word
Calming Angry Kids: Help and Hope for Parents in the Whirlwind
Trust the Stars (fiction)
The Kissing Bridge (fiction)
Beside Still Waters: A Big Sky Novel (fiction)
Breath of Bones (fiction, with Nathan Goyer)
Life, in Spite of Me (with Kristen Jane Anderson)

Leslie Nunnery is a prominent figure in the Christian homeschooling community. As the co-founder of *Teach Them Diligently*, she has dedicated herself to providing resources and experiences to strengthen Christian homeschooling families through Biblical Parenting and Excellent Home Education. Leslie is also an accomplished author, with several books on parenting and homeschooling to her name, including *Teach Them Diligently: Raising Children of Promise* and *Heart School: How Amazing Parents Become Excellent Home Educators*. In addition to her writing, she is a sought-after speaker and the host of the Teach Them Diligently podcast, where she shares her expertise and passion for educating and equipping parents to realize their call and execute it well.

Find out more about Teach Them Diligently Events, Membership, and Resources at https://teachthemdiligently.net/

Books by Leslie
Teach Them Diligently: Raising Children of Promise
Heart School: How Amazing Parents Become Excellent Home Educators

Made in the USA
Columbia, SC
14 June 2024